D0330508

This boo̲.̲ ... ..
commemorate the issuance of the
official Southern Paiute medal

March 15, 1972

and is limited to 15,000 copies
No. **5702**

Bill Som

Photograph by Robert C. Euler

THE PAIUTE COMMUNITY OF KAIBAB, present home of most of the Kaibab Paiute Indians, as seen on a beautiful summer day in 1971.

THE
PAIUTE
PEOPLE

by Robert C. Euler

Series Scientific Editors: Henry F. Dobyns & Robert C. Euler
General Editor: John I. Griffin

PUBLISHED BY INDIAN TRIBAL SERIES / PHOENIX

Library of Congress Catalog Number 70-188134

PRINTED IN THE UNITED STATES OF AMERICA — Imperial Lithographers

A STATEMENT
FROM THE TRIBAL CHAIRMAN

A S CHAIRMAN OF THE KAIBAB PAIUTE PEOPLE, I extend to you our personal thanks for your interest in our story — our past, our present and our hopes for the future.

Our home is located on the 'Kaibab Plateau', an area of the United States which provides little to its inhabitants. The land is for the most part unused, primarily because of a lack of sufficient supplies of water.

By your acquisition of our coin-medal and book issue, you have provided my people with hope for a better tomorrow. Funds received by the tribe from this issue will go toward financing an archaeological 'dig' on the reservation to unearth the secrets of a Pueblo ruin, last occupied hundreds of years ago.

We believe this ruin, once uncovered, will attract tourists in numbers large enough to provide employment and revenue for tribal members at projected tourist facilities near the site.

We look forward to the day when your travels will bring you to our land. . .the home of the Kaibab Paiute Indians.

Bill Tom

BILL TOM
Paiute Tribal Chairman

WHEN EUROPEAN EXPLORERS first traversed the canyonlands and plateaus of southern Utah and northern Arizona and the Great Basin of southeastern Nevada they made occasional contacts with small groups of Indians whom we have come to speak of as Southern Paiute. They found these Indians living in impermanent camps, hunting and gathering wild plants, and occasionally farming near permanent water courses throughout this broad territory.

The Southern Paiutes speak a language closely related to those spoken by many other Indians in the western portions of the United States and Mexico. This is the Numic language, so named after the Paiute name for themselves, *nüwü*, literally meaning person or human being. As with so many other American Indian tribes, the Southern Paiute considered themselves the only true humans on the earth. The Numic tongue is

1

further grouped by linguists into a Uto-Aztecan stock and thus it is allied to those spoken by such seemingly diverse peoples as the Cahuilla and Luiseño in southern California, the Tarahumara and Nahuatl in Mexico, the Hopi and Papago in Arizona, and the Ute in Colorado and Utah.

There is linguistic and archaeological evidence that these Numic speakers spread across the Great Basin into the northern portion of the Southwest some time shortly after A.D. 1000, replacing prehistoric Pueblo or Pueblo-like peoples who had earlier lived in the region. In extreme southern Nevada and southwestern Utah, archaeologists have excavated the distinctive ceramic remains of the Southern Paiute in direct association with those of the Pueblos made around A.D. 1150. The Paiute pottery was brown or reddish-brown, conical with pointed bottoms, and often decorated with rows of "finger nail" incisions. This is easily distinguished from the highly decorated black-on-white, black-on-yellow, or polychrome pottery of the Pueblos.

Along with pottery, archaeologists have uncovered milling stones, rectangular slabs the surfaces of which were roughened by pecking them with a harder stone. These were, and still are, used by the Paiute for pounding various wild food products such as seeds, pine nuts and meat as well as for "grinding" corn. Again, they

2

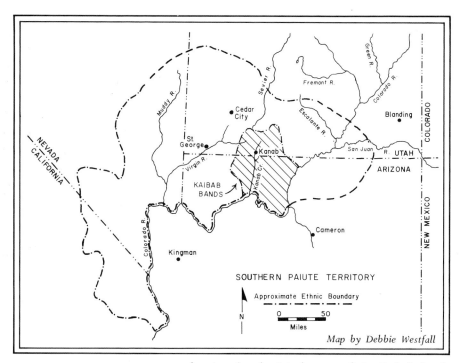

SOUTHERN PAIUTE TERRITORY showing the aboriginal range of the Kaibab band of northern Arizona.

are quite different from the troughed grinding stones of the Pueblo Indians.

Some of the Pueblo ruins in southern Nevada that were abandoned in the mid-twelfth century seem to have had defensive arrangements and it has been suggested that, as the Paiute moved into the area, there may have been increasing hostilities between the two groups, perhaps due to economic competition for scarce resources. While there is but limited evidence for the existence of this type of warfare, since such attacks would have left little if any trace for the archaeologists to uncover centuries later, the pressures may have been sufficient to cause the Pueblos to leave their homes and farms.

Be that as it may, the Paiutes probably learned how to farm corn, and perhaps beans and squash, during this period enabling them to begin at least a semi-sedentary existence.

Between A.D. 1300 and 1600 there is additional evidence of contact between the Southern Paiute and the Pueblo Hopi Indians in the southern parts of Paiute territory, especially on the north side of the Grand Canyon. During these centuries, however, the relationships between the two tribes seem to have been amicable. The Paiute were simply trading their products for the beautiful black-on-yellow pottery of the Hopis.

During all these years the Southern Paiute must have been expanding their territory eastward. By the year of America's independence, when we have the first historic record of these Indians, they were living in a great crescentic region from southeastern Utah and northeastern Arizona to the deserts of southern California and Nevada.

THE SPANISH HISTORICAL PERIOD

The historic period for the Southern Paiute, if not their first contact with Europeans, began on the 10th of October, 1776. In southern Utah, a few miles north of the present community of Cedar City, a small party of Spanish explorers encountered about twenty Indians who had been gathering grass seeds. The Spaniards, led by Father Francisco Atanasio Dominguez and Father Silvestre Velez de Escalante, in the company of eight other men, had left Santa Fe almost three months perviously to look for a feasible overland route to the missions in California. The southern route as well as that through northern Arizona was considered too hazardous because of hostile Apache and Hopi Indians. The expedition, mounted and driving a small herd of cattle for provisions, had gone north, past Mesa Verde in southwestern Colorado and into Utah as far north as Utah Lake. Here they acquired a Ute Indian guide. Experiencing more difficulties than they had anticipated and being concerned about the forthcoming winter, the party reluctantly aban-

Courtesy Peabody Museum, Harvard University
SOUTHERN PAIUTE POTTERY bowl showing typical fingernail incisions. Collected by Edward Palmer from Kaibab Paiutes in 1875.

Photograph by Robert C. Euler
SOUTHERN PAIUTE MILLING STONE and mano used on the Shivwits Paiute Reservation as late as 1962.

doned its plans and turned south to return to Santa Fe. So it was that they entered the territory of the Paiute, whom they called "Payuchis," on that fall day. Escalante was the chronicler of the expedition while an engineer and retired captain of militia, Don Bernardo Miera y Pacheco, was in charge of astronomical records and map making. From the journal and the illuminating map, the great historian, Herbert Eugene Bolton, was able to retrace the route of this intrepid party and provide a readily available translation of the first written record of the Southern Paiute.

When they met the Indian seed gathering party, the explorers forcibly detained some of the women. Frightened, the Indians attempted to flee, but later told Escalante that there were many of their people in the vicinity. These women were wearing "only some pieces of buckskin hanging from their waists" although Escalante noted that "the Payuchis traded only for red clothes," an indication that they had been in some contact, probably indirectly, with Europeans before 1776.

That same day a Paiute man was brought to the Spaniards' camp. He, too, was extremely frightened but at last conversed with the Ute interpreter. When questioned about a large "hemp" net that he was carrying, the Paiute said that it was for catching rabbits. He had traded it and some colored shells from "other Indians

8

Photograph Courtesy Robert C. Euler

THE AUTHOR examining the historic ruins of a Southern Paiute wickiup on the Indian Peak Paiute Reservation. When these brush structures collapsed and disintegrated, the only remaining surface evidence is a circular depression of stones and charred poles.

who live down the Rio Grande. . .", that being the Spaniards' designation for the Colorado River. In all probability, this external trade was carried on with Mohave, Hopi, or Havasupai Indians to the south.

Just south of Cedar City, Escalante's party was taken to a Paiute camp inhabited by their guide, two other men, three women, and several children. Given the relatively sparse natural food resources of the region, this was probably an average population for a Paiute camp and may have constituted an extended family of several related adults. Escalante noted that the Indians "had very good piñon nuts, dates [the fruit of the yucca plant], and some little sacks of maize."

The Spaniards gave a hunting knife and some glass beads to one of the Indians in exchange for which two of them led the explorers south to Ash Creek. Here the guides fled into the mountains but the party continued into the valley. Here, Escalante remarked:

"The Indians who live in the valley and in its vicinity to the west, north, and east are called in their language Huascari. They dress very poorly, and eat grass seeds, hares, piñon nuts in season, and dates. They do not plant maize, and judging from what we saw, they obtain very little of it. They are extremely cowardly. . ."

The Spanish friar was undoubtedly referring to the Southern Paiute although the term *Huascari*

11

apparently has no Paiute equivalent. The frequent references to these Indians as being cowardly were undoubtedly the result of their apprehension upon meeting mounted Europeans for the first time.

That the Paiute were farming corn, however, was noted in Escalante's journal a day or two later. Continuing south toward the Virgin River near St. George, Utah, the party

"found a well made mat with a large supply of ears and husks of green corn which had been placed on it. Near it, in the small plain and on the bank of the river, there were three small corn patches with their very well made irrigation ditches. .,.From here downstream and on the mesas on either side for a long distance, according to what we learned, live Indians who sustain themselves by planting maize and calabashes, and who in their language are called the Parussi."

Parussi is the Paiute name for the Virgin River, "white river," because it foamed as it went through a canyon. Since the Paiute local groups usually went by names referring to a nearby geographic feature, the *Parussi* were those Southern Paiute living along lower Ash Creek and at its junction with the Virgin.

After the Spanish priests had crossed the Virgin, they met eight more Paiutes who offered for trade some strings of *"chalchihuite,"* or turquoise, "each string having a colored shell."

12

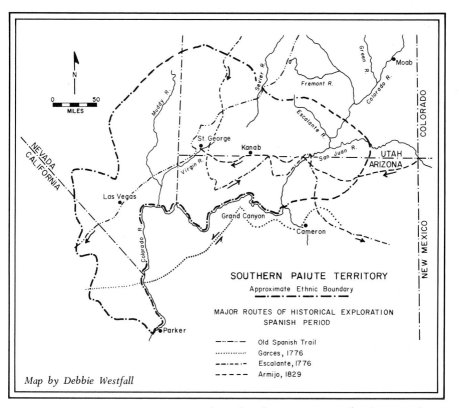

ROUTES OF SPANISH EXPLORATION through the country of the Southern Paiute.

These necklaces probably had been obtained from the Hopi.

A few days later, some twenty miles north of Mount Trumbull, the Escalante party entered some of the most isolated of all Southern Paiute lands. Here they encountered five more Indians, at least one of whom had a bow and arrows. In exchange for a piece of woolen cloth, three of them led the Spaniards to water and then promised them food, "a small supply of wild [mountain] sheep, dried tuna [prickly pear cactus fruit] made into cakes, and grass seeds." The following day, twenty of these Indians came into the explorers' camp "with some cakes or loaves of tuna and several bags of the seeds of various herbs" to barter. Later, many more Indians came in with "many bags of the seeds mentioned and some fresh tunas. . .and dried ones made into cakes." They informed Escalante that "they were called Yubuincariris and that they did not plant maize; that their foods were seeds, tunas, piñon nuts. . .and what hares, rabbits and wild sheep they hunted." These hunting and gathering Indians were Uinkarets Paiute, people of the "pine sitting place," which is what they called Mount Trumbull.

By now the Spaniards realized that they were headed too far south, toward the Grand Canyon, which they could not cross. So they turned northeast toward what later became known as the Crossing of the Fathers in the Glen Canyon

15

of the Colorado River. This brought them to the territory of the Kaibab group of Southern Paiute with whom they made contact just east of the present town of Kanab, Utah. One night they saw fires and soon came upon "three little Indian huts." The Paiutes who were camped there gave the hungry explorers some piñon nuts and rabbit meat. The elderly engineer, Don Bernardo Miera y Pacheco, had become ill and, interestingly, a Paiute medicine man tried to cure him "with songs and ceremonies." Father Escalante permitted this reluctantly but later scolded the Indians for their "superstitions."

Apparantly there were other Paiute camps nearby because all that day Indians kept coming in to see the Spaniards. Escalante preached to twenty-six of them and they told him about other Indian tribes, the Moquinos and the Cosninas. These were the Hopi and the Havasupai respectively, with whom the Paiute had trading relationships.

After a difficult crossing of the Colorado River at a point that is now under the waters of Lake Powell behind Glen Canyon Dam, the Dominguez-Escalante party saw more Paiute camps but were unable to converse with their inhabitants. From there they soon left Paiute territory and returned to the New Mexico pueblo of Zuñi by way of the Hopi villages.

The Escalante journal has been discussed at some length because it recorded the initial

16

meeting of Europeans with Southern Paiute. It also, of course, gives the first written account about the aboriginal life of these Indians. From an interpretation of it in anthropological more than in historical terms it is clear that the Paiute ranged over a wide expanse of land, environmentally quite varied. Throughout this region, the Indians depended for food primarily upon wild plants such as grass seeds and cactus fruits and upon their skill in hunting rabbits and mountain sheep. These they took with bows and arrows or, in the case of rabbits, with long nets. Everywhere that Escalante met them they were living in small, probably temporary camps except along the permanent streams where they farmed corn and squash and lived a more sedentary life. The diary even includes a glimpse of native religion in the curing ceremony that the Paiutes attempted for Captain Miera.

In the same year that Dominguez and Escalante were travelling through Utah, another Franciscan priest, Father Francisco Garcés, was exploring farther to the west, in Arizona and California into the Mohave Desert. While Garcés, who was stationed at the mission of San Xavier del Bac near Tucson, did not cross the Colorado River into Utah, he did visit the most southwestern of all Southern Paiute groups, a tribe now known as the Chemehuevi, living near the Mohave Indians along the lower Colorado and in the desert to the west.

In the early summer of 1776, Father Garcés was making his lonely way through the desert not too far south of the present town of Needles, California. There he "met some 40 persons of the Chemebet nation" who, he reporteded in his journal, were wearing moccasins, shirts of antelope skin, white headdresses "like a cap...with a bunch of those very curious feathers which certain birds of this country have in their crest..." All the Indians were carrying "a crook besides their weapons." Garcés made it clear that the Chemehuevi, in the 18th century anyway, did not distinguish themselves from the Southern Paiute in the Las Vegas, Nevada, area immediately to the north.

In the decades following the Dominguez – Escalante expedition, a number of Spanish trading parties probably made contact with the Southern Paiute. Although there is but indirect evidence for these, it is evident that a flourishing, albeit illegal, slave trade developed. Spaniards originating in Santa Fe traveled northwest along what came to be known as the Old Spanish Trail into the territory of the Ute. These more powerful Indians had begun raids upon the impoverished Paiute and carried off children whom they later bartered to the Spaniards.

One such party, commanded by Mauricio Arzé and Lagos Garcia, left Abiquiu north of Santa Fe in March of 1813. Ultimately reaching the Sanpete Utes, who incidentally wore heavy beards, the traders were met with some hostility. Returning through the country of other Utes, Arzé and Garcia obtained twelve slaves whom they took to Santa Fe. Similar slave trading parties continued to travel into Paiute territory well into the nineteenth century.

THE ANGLO HISTORICAL EXPLORATIONS

Although fur traders, in the period after 1813, coursed up the Green and Uintah rivers of Utah, none apparently traveled west as far as Southern Paiute country. However, in 1826 and 1827, the trapper Jedediah Smith made two notable explorations through Paiute territory and was the first to link the earlier routes of Escalante and Garcés. Smith had come west in 1822 to trap furs for William H. Ashley and, before he was killed by Comanches in 1831, he saw more of the west than any explorer before him. Indeed, he was the first to travel throughout all of the Great Basin.

Coming south from the Great Salt Lake in August of 1826, Smith traded with the Ute Indians of Utah Valley and then proceeded up the Sevier River. Cutting over the mountains to Cove Fort, Smith made little mention in his journal of Indians until he was well within the Southern Paiute range near the junction of Santa Clara Creek and the Virgin River just west of present St. George. Here, according to his diary, he "fell in with a nation of Indians who call themselves *Pa-Ulches...*who raise some little corn and pumpkins. The country is nearly destitute of game of any description except a few hares." These Paiutes, who were wearing rabbit skin robes, had "marble" pipes and "flint" knives, received the American explorer on friendly terms. Continuing his lonely way westerly, Smith also met some Paiute farming on Beaver Dam Wash, which he called "Pautch Creek."

Then, following a tortuous route through the canyons of the Virgin and the Colorado, Smith finally reached the Mohave Indian villages near present day Needles. He described these sedentary Indians, southerly neighbors of the Paiute, as follows: "I here found a nation of Indians who call themselves Ammuchábas; they cultivate the soil, and raise corn, beans, pumkins [*sic.*], watermelons and muskmelons in abundance, and also a little wheat and cotton." Apparently the Mohave already had obtained melon seeds and wheat from the Spaniards, probably those from the California missions. After remaining with these river Indians for fifteen days, on November 10th, 1826, Smith, guided by two Mission Indians, went west across the Mohave Desert. For another fifteen days he traveled "over a country of complete barrens" and did not mention any Indians resembling the Paiute or the Chemehuevi.

20

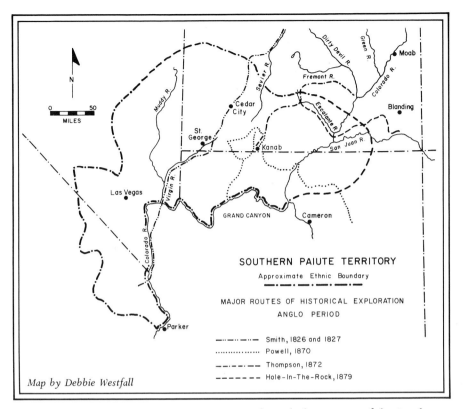

ROUTES OF ANGLO-AMERICAN EXPLORATION through the country of the Southern Paiute.

The following year, Jed Smith repeated the trip and again met Paiute farming near the mouth of the Virgin. At the Mohave villages he surprisingly found these Indians hostile and, after a fight during his crossing of the Colorado River, he continued west up the Mohave River, which he aptly named the "Inconstant." There he wrote: "About 8 miles up the river I found 2 horses and soon after 2 indian lodges...I found them to be Pauch..." At the Paiute camp, which was probably Chemehuevi, Smith traded cloth, knives, and beads for "their horses, some cane grass candy and some demi jons for carrying water."

Although Smith gave some accurate, albeit sketchy information about the Paiutes for the 1826-1827 period, all of his original maps of the country seem to have been lost. The earliest dated map so far located which seems to have been based on the originals made by Smith, is one published in Parish in 1833 and was drawn by the erudite French cartographer, A. H. Brue. Smith's influence is evident since Brue used the American trapper's names for the rivers of the area: Ashley for the Sevier, Adams for the Virgin, and Seeds-Keeder for the Green and the Colorado. In 1834, Brue published a similar map on which he attempted to show Smith's route of travel, but there is no evidence that either of these was based on sketches by Smith himself. Brue's 1834 map showed the Pa-Utches south of

23

Salt Lake on the Adams (Virgin) River, and the Ammuchiebes (Mohave) on the Seeds-Keeder (Colorado), but did not refer to the Chemehuevi. The Paiute, incidentally, were noted on this map as "cultivateurs." Another map showing Smith's trails, was published in 1839 by David H. Burr, Geographer to the U. S. House of Representatives. One of Smith's biographers, Maurice Sullivan, believed that "the far western part of this map is so nearly accurate that it must have been copied from a sketch by Smith himself, or based on Smith's notes." This showed the "Pa-U-Teh" in the area of the Adams (Virgin) River, but did not locate either the Mohave or the Chemehuevi.

It is important to note that Jedediah Smith's contact with the Southern Paiute was, like that of the Escalante party a full half century earlier, a friendly one. Even after his ambush by the Mohaves, an event about which the Paiute probably learned, Smith reported no Paiute hostilities on either trip. This, however, is not so surprising as the fact that Smith was able to spend fifteen days with the Mohave in late October and early November of 1826. For, earlier that year, in mid-March, another fur trapper, the blustering James Ohio Pattie had precipitated two attacks on the Mohave as he trapped and tramped through their Colorado River villages. After Pattie's party had killed Papago Indians on the Gila River of Arizona

24

earlier that spring, a Mohave chief demanded a horse in payment for the beaver the trappers had taken. When it wasn't forthcoming, the Indian speared a horse, whereupon Pattie's men killed him. Word of this hostility probably soon spread to neighboring Indian tribes, including Paiute and Walapai, and this may well have led to later enmity between Anglo-Americans and Indians in those regions.

Pattie's journal is confusing and demonstrably untrustworthy, but it does seem possible that after the unfortunate episode in the Mohave villages, the trappers proceeded farther up the Colorado River where, three days later, on March 16th, they "came upon a small party [of Indians], of whom the men fled, leaving a single woman. Seeing herself in our power, she began to beat her breast, and cry *Cowera, Cowera;* from which we gathered that she belonged to that tribe." This woman may simply have been uttering a word of fear or apprehension in her native tongue. If, however, the term "Cowera" referred to her tribal affiliation, she may have been a Paiute. Father Garces, in 1776, had referred to a "Chemebet Quajalas" north of the Mohave. These same people were called Cahual-chitz by the Yuma Indians who, in 1849 also placed them north of the Mohaves. In 1858 an American Army officer, Lieutenant J. L. White, referred to them as Cohualch. This sounds similar to Kohoaldje, the Mohave Indian name for the Virgin River Paiutes. This meeting between the Pattie party and the Indian woman probably took place near or just south of the confluence of the Virgin River with the Colorado.

A week later, if we can believe Pattie's journal, the trappers were continuing up the Colorado. There, in his words: "We came to a village of the Shuena Indians. As we approached it, they came out and began to fire arrows upon us. We gave them in return a round of rifle balls." These Shuena Indians probably were a band of Paiute known as Shivwits. If so, their brief battle with the Pattie party marks their first antagonism toward white men.

More trappers and traders crossed portions of Southern Paiute territory in 1829 and 1830, but their accounts unfortunately reveal little about the Indians they met. In 1829, for example, some trappers under the leadership of Ewing Young and guided by Kit Carson went from Taos, New Mexico, to San Gabriel in California via the Mohave settlements but mentioned no Indians resembling Paiute or Chemehuevi. That same year, a notorious trapper, Thomas "Pegleg" Smith, was searching for beaver on the Santa Clara and Virgin rivers; again, he made no reference to Indians.

The year 1829 also saw a party of Hudson's Bay Company trappers, led by Peter Skene Ogden, on the Old Spanish Trail. In the fall of that year they came down to Sevier Lake, and in February arrived on the Virgin. From there they went on to the Mohave villages and, after a skirmish with those Indians, continued over the route west along the Mohave River to the California mountains.

In the late fall of 1830, George C. Yount, who had been with Pattie four years earlier, and William Wolfskill, led the first party to go over the entire distance of the longer route of the Old Spanish Trail. The two men had been traders in Santa Fe in the 1820's and, before 1830, Yount had twice been among the Mohave and into the Great Salt Lake Valley. Although Yount did not dictate his account of the trip until twenty-five years later, it has some rather startling things to say about the Southern Paiute. The party encountered its first Paiute somewhere near the south end of the Sevier Valley, the precise location not being determinable. Here they met "a solitary Indian. . .a single rabbit-skin hung over his otherwise nakid [sic.] shoulders. . . With a rude bow and arrows he was hunting rabbits. . ." This Indian led the white men to his people whom Yount described as:

"a groupe [sic.] of the lowest & most degraded of all the savage hords [sic.] of the west. . . All they had in the world was some dried rabbit-meat. . . They had not a hatchet, nor any instrument to cut or perforate the softest wood. . . They would get fire by rubbing

27

together pieces of hard wood. . .When they would fell a tree for fuel, or for any purpose they built a fire about its roots — & they cut it up with fire — To erect a dwellinghouse for their own abode & shield them from the severe cold, they were accustomed to break off boughs & stick them in the snow & sloping the tops inward they would pile bushes on top. . .The name of their tribe is *Piuch*. . .They have but few words & communicate chiefly by signs — They live in little clans scattered over a very great extent of country — A traveller who has been among them within a few months [1855 when the narrative was recorded] informs us that they have now become the most adroit thieves in the world — Their food consists of occasionally a Rabbit, with roots & mice, grasshoppers & insects, such as flies, spiders & worms of every kind — Where nuts exist they gather them for food — They also luxuriate & grow fat when they find a patch of clover — On many kinds of grass they feed like cattle — They love to be covered with lice because they appropriate these for food."

Analysis of the Yount contacts with the Paiute is difficult. Obviously, they exhibited the typically ethnocentric attitude of Anglo-American trappers and traders of their day. To indicate, for example, that the Paiute language contained few words was an indication of a stereotyped view of non-literate people that, unfortunately, all too many white people maintain today. Since this description of the Paiute and their country is much more bleak and

28

TAPEATS, A Kaibab Paiute, photographed near St. George, Utah, in 1872.

foreboding than those of earlier explorers, one wonders if the time of this observation — late fall with snow on the ground — might not have followed a particularly acute drought period. Or, events that took place in the twenty-five years between the trip and the recording of the narrative might have biased Yount's cultural viewpoint.

In any event, he did record something about Paiute culture, a way of life which was still essentially aboriginal. Yount and Wolfskill saw the Paiute wearing rabbit fur robes; eating dried rabbit meat, roots, mice, and insects; felling trees by fire; and making crude "wikiups" from tree limbs. Yount's remark that the Paiute were eating lice is doubtful; more likely the Indians were merely killing them by cracking them in their teeth. Although the account of this contact is brief, biased, and temporally distant, it nevertheless appears that the Paiute whom these traders saw had received few if any Anglo-American material goods. They were continuing a marginal subsistence pattern, moving about their territory in what probably were small extended family groups. It is also evident that they were not disposed to attack the well-armed trappers.

Commercial traffic over the Old Spanish Trail through Southern Paiute territory began about this same time. The first pack train was taken by a New Mexican, Antonio Armijo, over a shortened route, generally westward, along what later became the Arizona-Utah state border. Armijo sent a preliminary report of their expedition to Mexico City where it was published under the title "Route Discovered from the Village of Abiquiu in the Territory of New Mexico to Upper California." In this, Armijo said of the Paiute: "The gentiles of the Payuche nation inhabit the vicinity of the ...[Colorado]... river; their living quarters are *jacales,* and they live on grass seeds, hares and rabbits, using the skins of the latter to cover a small part of their body." A few days later, on June 19, 1830, Armijo's very terse diary was published in the *Registro Oficial del Gobierno de los Estados-Unidos Mexicanos* (Official Government Register of the United States of Mexico). This revealed that, rather than taking the more roundabout route up to the Sevier River, the Armijo train made straight for the place of Escalante's return crossing of the Colorado — the Crossing of the Fathers. Near "the Navajo Mountain we found another settlement of Navajos. . ." Armijo noted. This was not the present Navajo Mountain astride the Utah-Arizona border, but a landmark considerably south of the San Juan River and to the east. It was not until two days later that Armijo came to. . ."the little canyon of Chelli Creek." This was Canyon de Chelly in northeastern Arizona near the New Mexico state line. Five days later, probably near Paiute Canyon, the party arrived "at the water hole of the *Payuches:* three Indians were found, no trouble ensued. . ." This would certainly indicate that, in 1830, Paiutes were still ranging considerably to the south and east, in what is now northern Arizona. At this point, Armijo and his pack mules must have encountered some difficulty skirting Navajo Mountain and the rough canyons flanking it, because it took him six days more to reach the Crossing of the Fathers. Two additional days were spent by the packers climbing up the far side of the river before they could again turn west toward present-day Kanab. About a day before reaching the Paria River, "there was found a settlement of Payuches, with no mishap; it is a gentle and cowardly nation." No further mention of Paiutes was made by Armijo until the expedition reached the mouth of what is probably Las Vegas Wash, when he saw ". . .villages of the *Cucha Payuches* and the *Hayatas.*" The latter were undoubtedly Mohave (the Paiute word for them is *ayat*) and Armijo was then just at the northern edge of their range. Six days later, possibly on the Amargosa River, Armijo recorded: "At the River of the Payuches. . .a village was found: nothing happened for it was gentle." Armijo arrived at San Gabriel on January 31st, 1830, and returned to Santa Fe by the same route in March of that year although he apparently left no written

32

record of that homeward bound trip. Although Armijo's journal was all too brief, its notes on the Paiute not only provide information about the territory over which these Indians were ranging, but also corroborated the Yount account of their impoverished and peaceful character.

From 1830 on, commercial traffic over the Old Spanish Trail apparently was relatively heavy. However, the traders seemed not to be inclined toward record keeping. No journals of the regular annual merchant trains of 1831 to 1848 have been located.

Nonetheless, two or three other accounts of the pre-1848 period give some space to the Paiute. In the summer of 1839, Thomas J. Farnham traveled through portions of their territory. Of the Paiutes in the Sevier River region he remarked:

"Between this river [the Colorado] and the Great Salt Lake, there is a stream called Severe River, which rises in the high plateaux to the S.E. of the lake..,.Here live the 'Piutes' and 'Lank Pitches,' the most degraded and least intellectual Indians known to the trappers. They wear no clothing of any description – build no shelters. They eat roots, lizards, and snails... They provide nothing for future wants. And when the lizards and snails and wild roots are buried in the snows of winter, they are said to retire to the vicinity of timber, dig holes in the form of ovens in the steep sides of the sand hills and having heated themselves to a certain degree, deposit themselves in them, and sleep fast until the weather permits them to go abroad again and hunt for food.''

In a slightly later volume, Farnham further described the Paiutes in these terms: "The northern banks of the Colorado, the region of Severe River, and those portions of the Timpanigos desert where man can find a snail to eat, are inhabited by a race of Indians...Piutes." He also extensively quoted from an account given him by a Dr. Lyman, who journeyed over the Old Spanish Trail in 1841:

"...yet this immense tract of country is inhabited by a comparatively numerous tribe of Indians, generally known as the Paiuches, but by some called the Shoshonies, a name perhaps more properly applied to a tribe living a few degrees to the northward, and very much like the Paiuches in character.

"The Paiuches speak the same language as the Yutas, and are a branch of that tribe...The food of these Indians is in conformity with the character of the country they inhabit. They collect the seeds of grasses, growing on the margins of the springs and salt ponds, roast and pulverize them between two stones, and then boil them into a thick mush...Sometimes they succeed in ensnaring a hare, the flesh of which they eat, and the skin of which they cut into cords with the fur adhering; and braid them together so as to form a sort of cloak with a hole in the middle, through which they thrust their

34

Smithsonian Institution National Anthropological Archives, Neg. No. 1610.
AN ELDERLY KAIBAB PAIUTE WOMAN weaving a basket in front of her wikiup
in 1872. The variety of basket forms was common in Paiute camps.

heads. The bark of pine trees growing on some of the trap mountains, is also a general article of food; so are roots! Ants, grasshoppers, and lizards, are classed among their choicest dainties! "They. .,.make some weapons of defence... The bows are about six feet long; made of the savine [Juniper]...Their arrows are made of a species of cane-bamboo...three to four feet long, pointed with a bit of fire-hardened wood ...Their habitations...are of the rudest character. Some of them are mere holes dug in the sand-hills; others consist of sticks and branches of brush and trees piled up conically, and covered with dirt. This latter kind is usually found where they attempt villages of greater or less size, and stand huddled closely together."

These accounts, like that of Yount, are so biased, indicating the ethnocentric values held by Anglo-Americans of the time, that they require some interpretation. Because of these values, the explorers were totally unable to comprehend the nature of Southern Paiute life ways. They were repelled by what they considered to be some sort of "animal-like" behavior. Even if we discount the improbable tale of Paiutes hibernating in the winter, it is still clear that Farnham and his contemporaries were simply echoing attitudes expressed by their countrymen of the period. At the same time, if these obviously skewed reports are interpreted, evaluated, by anthropologists skilled in a cross-cultural, objective approach to understanding

36

the behavior of all peoples, at all times, and in all places, some valid aspects of Paiute culture stand out.

It is obvious, for example, that the American travelers encountered Paiutes living in a marginal portion of their territory. With years of experience in coping with a somewhat hostile environment, the Paiutes apparently were in total ecological tune with the plant and animal food resources available to them. They survived while the American explorers were often on the verge of starvation.

In addition, the Farnham and Lyman journals, when analyzed realistically, reveal other aspects of Paiute life. The skill required to produce a warm and serviceable rabbit fur robe, the expertise required to know and locate *edible* seeds and roots, the ability to understand the physics of the bow and arrow and to produce functional weapons of this type, all point to the rapport that the Paiutes enjoyed with their culture and their environment.

Yet, the derogatory accounts of them continued. In 1841, the French priest, Father deSmet, wrote:

"The *Sampectches*, the *Payouts*, and the *Ampayouts* are the nearest neighbors of the *Serpents*. Probably in all the world there is not another people more wretched, more disreputable, or more poverty-stricken. The French usually call them the *Dignes-de-pitie* [Worthy of pity], a very appropriate name. The country they inhabit is really a heath; they live in the crevices of rocks or in holes dug into the ground; they have no clothing; their armor consists entirely of a bow, some arrows, and a pointed stick; they run over the uncultivated land in search of ants and grass-hoppers, which they eat; and if they find a few tasteless roots or some evil-smelling grain, they consider it a real feast. Reliable persons have informed me that they eat the bodies of their near relatives [the translation can also mean neighbors] and that sometimes they even eat their own children. Since one seldom sees more than two, three, or four of them at the same time, it is impossible to know how many of them there are. They are so timid that a stranger would have difficulty in approaching them. As soon as they see someone, be he white or Indian, they raise an alarm (wood smoke); an instant later, the same signal is multiplied wherever any of their people are found. As more than four hundred of them have been seen at once, running to hide in inaccessible rocks at this signal, it may be presumed that they are very numerous. When they are hunting for roots or ants, they hide their small children in the grass or in holes in the rocks. Occasionally some of them dare to leave their hiding places, seek out white people, and trade them their children for trifles. Sometimes the Spanish from California make excursions into their country in order to capture and carry away their children. I have been assured that they treat these children kindly, give them religious instruction, and when they reach a certain age either set them free or keep them in a kind of servitude, making them care for the horses or work on the farms. I have had the satisfaction of baptizing several of these unfortunate beings; they too have told me the same things that I have related. It would be easy to find guides among these new converts; by this means one could introduce himself among these poor forsaken people, teach them the consoling tidings of the Gospel, and render their fate, if not happier on earth, at least better by the hope of a future of eternal happiness."

The French priest's report also cannot be taken at face value. He, too, was relying upon the accounts of others to supplement his own slightly distant views. He certainly was not intimately acquainted with the Paiute or their immediate habitat.

That the Paiute, however, were a shy, apprehensive people has been documented in the earlier Spanish journals. But, the expeditions of slave traders among them may well have accounted for their seemingly "cowardly" nature. During the 1830's and 1840's, and even continuing into the 1850's, slaving expeditions came into the Paiute country from California and Santa Fe. While most accounts failed to differentiate between Indians, i.e., Paiute from Ute, some referred directly to the Paiute. Kit Carson, while accompanying Fremont's second expedition in Ute territory east of the Wasatch Mountains "bought an Indian boy of about twelve to fourteen years for forty dollars. He belongs to the Paiute Nation, which subsists only on mice, locusts, and roots, and such a life as the present must please him very much." One James A. Bennett, writing in his diary from Santa Fe about Southern Utah on January 3, 1851, said: "I was surprised to learn that the Pi Utah Indians, also known as Ant Eaters or Root Diggers are brought here every spring and sold as slaves." Bennett also noted that Paiute slaves brought from $100 to $400 on the Santa Fe market. His reference to the Paiute should be taken with caution, however, since he also remarked that "these Indians are found in the neighborhood of the Gila River," in southern Arizona and much too far south for Paiute.

The expedition of Lieutenant Edward F. Beale in 1853 saw frightened Indians on the Santa Clara River in southwestern Utah and the officer noted: "Yearly expeditions are fitted out in New Mexico to trade with the Pah-Utahs for their children..." Daniel W. Jones, a Utah pioneer, wrote in 1851 about Walker's band of Ute that "were in the habit of raiding on the Pahutes..." for children. John D. Lee, writing from Harmony in southern Utah on February 5, 1853, told of a band of Utes under the same chief Walker attacking some "Piedes" of the region in the preceding month. And, in December of 1854, Jacob Hamblin advised the Salt Lake City Mormon newspaper, the *Deseret News,* that Sanpitch, a brother of Chief Wakara,

A KAIBAB PAIUTE SUMMER CAMP in 1872. Two of the women are wearing basketry caps while one is grinding food on a milling stone. A young girl is holding a baby in a cradle board. The bow and quiver of arrows and the conical burden baskets are typical of this period.

went to the Piutes on the Santa Clara for trading and slaving. As late as 1860, Dr. Garland Hurt, Indian agent in Utah, wrote: "Between the Utahs proper and the Py-eeds there is a species of traffic. . .bartering of children. So abject and degraded are the Py-eeds that they will sell their children to the Utahs for a few trinkets or bits of clothing."

Even discounting the alleged "abjectness and degradation" of the Southern Paiute of 1860, it would be valuable to know for how long and how early they had been subject to slave raids. Such raids might account in large part for their timidity even during the early Spanish explorations.

These traits, however, seem not applicable to the Paiutes of southwestern Utah in 1844. In that year the first American military party passed over the Old Spanish Trail. This was the second expedition of Brevet Captain John C. Fremont on his return from Oregon and California in the spring of the year. Traveling eastward he failed to identify Indians until he was on the Mojave River near the present town of Daggett, California. Here, on April 23rd, he remarked:

"Here a party of six Indians came into camp, poor and hungry. . .Their arms were bows of unusual length, and each had a large gourd, strengthened with meshes of cord, in which he carried water. . .They proved to be the Mohahve

42

Indians. . .sometimes called Amuchaba. . .He [one who spoke Spanish] said they lived upon a large river in the southeast, which the 'soldiers called the Rio Colorado'; but that formerly, a portion of them lived upon this river, and among the mountains which had bounded the river valley to the northward during the day, and that here along the river they had raised various kinds of melons. They sometimes came over to trade with the Indians of the Sierra [California], bringing with them blankets and goods manufactured by the Monquis [Hopi] and other Colorado Indians. They rarely carried home horses, on account of the difficulty of getting them across the desert, and of guarding them afterwards from the Pa-Utah Indians, who inhabit the Sierra, at the head of the Rio Virgen. . ."

As Fremont continued eastward from this encounter, nine days later, "Many *digger* [a term Fremont used for the Paiute] tracks are seen around us but no Indians were visible." The following day the party camped at "*las Vegas*" and, one day later, on "the *Rio de los Angeles* [the Muddy River]. . .a branch of the *Rio Virgen*. . .Indians crowded numerously around us in the morning. . .Some. . .were on the bottoms, and others haranguing us from the bluffs; and they were scattered in every direction over the hills." For the first time since Pattie's trip, the Southern Paiute seem to have been bordering upon hostile retaliation of Anglo-American travels through their country.

43

Charles Preuss, the German cartographer with the Fremont expedition, also recorded in his journal of May 5, 1844, this incident on the Muddy: "We are much bothered by Paiutes. It is still doubtful where those murderers of the Spaniards [Mexicans whom Kit Carson and Alexander Godey, Fremont's guides, had avenged on April 27th] belong to this nation." Preuss, incidentally, also noted that "where wood is so scarce, the Indians make a sort of torch from the dry bark of sagebrush and carry the fire from one place to the other" and that "these Indians here are regular lizard eaters."

Fremont told more about this Paiute food habit: "Many of the Indians had long sticks, hooked at the end, which they used in hauling out lizards, and other small animals, from their holes. During the day they occasionally roasted and ate lizards at our fires. These belong to the people who are generally known under the name of *Diggers*. . ." The following day the party left "the *Rio de los Angeles,* and continued our way through the same desolate and revolting country, where lizards were the only animal, and the tracks of the lizard eaters the principal sign of human beings." Coming to the Virgin, "For several days we continued our journey up the river. . .and the sandy soil was absolutely covered with the tracks of Diggers." Here, on May 10th, one of Fremont's men was killed by the Paiute. As Preuss recorded it: "Only a mile

Smithsonian Institution National Anthropological Archives, Neg. No. 1608
A KAIBAB PAIUTE MAN flaking a stone knife in front of his wikiup in 1872.

from camp he was killed with arrows by hidden Indians and thrown into a rapid river...May God have mercy on the Paiutes who fall into our hands now. They lurk like wolves between the rocks along the road. Often we are surrounded by thirty or fifty of them without knowing it." After this incident, the Indians certainly were more circumspect. As Fremont himself noted: "The day before, they infested our camp; now, not one appeared; nor did we ever afterwards see but one who even belonged to the same tribe, and he at a distance."

It is quite probable that the Paiutes killed the white man because he interfered with their attempts to kill one of Fremont's horses for food. The murdered man had left the main party in search of a missing horse whom Carson and Godey later found wounded by an arrow. While this attempt to augment their meager food supply may not have been the sole reason for the Paiute hostility, it most certainly was a contributing factor.

The Fremont expedition then proceeded up the Santa Clara River in southwestern Utah to Sevier Lake and then northward for several days. "We met, in this traverse," Fremont noted, "a few mounted Utah Indians, in advance of their main body..." Thus did the Pathfinder distinguish "Diggers," the unmounted Paiute, from the "Utah," the horse-riding Ute Indians north of Sevier Lake. His 1844 map, illustrating this,

46

showed "Pah-Utah" Indians in the general vicinity of the Virgin River and "Utah" Indians west of Sevier Lake.

It may be worthwhile to note that elsewhere Fremont made some pertinent but general remarks on environmental conditions in the country of the Southern Paiute:

"Black tailed deer and mountain sheep are frequent in these mountains; which in consideration of their grass, water and wood, and the alluvion at their base, may be called fertile. . . Sterility, on the contrary, is the absolute characteristic of the valleys. . .no wood, no water, no grass; the gloomy artemisia [sage brush] the prevailing shrub — no animals, except the hares, which shelter in these shrubs, and the fleet and timid antelope. . .But few Indians are found, and those in the lowest state of human existence; living not even in communities, but in the elementary state of families, and sometimes a single individual to himself — except about the lakes stocked with fish, which become the property and resort of a small tribe."

The controversial explorer at least gave a somewhat more accurate account of the food resources that were exploited by the Southern Paiute in the central portion of their range.

Kit Carson, who had been over the western portion of the Old Spanish Trail with the Ewing Young trapping party in 1829, and later with Fremont, was, in the late 1840's, a dispatch bearer over the route. On one of his trips, in

1847, he also attested to the large numbers of Paiutes on the Muddy River in southeastern Nevada. On one trip he reported seeing "about 300 Indians" there. The following year, on a journey from west to east with George Brewerton, after crossing the Mohave Desert and approaching Las Vegas, Carson said: "The Pau-Eutaw or Digger Indians first made their appearance..." Farther east, on the Virgin River, Carson shot and killed a lone Paiute. Northward, "not far from Little Salt Lake the travellers met their first Utah Indians, under the leadership of Chief Wakara." Given the numbers of Paiute concentrated along the Muddy and Virgin in the 1840's, it is quite probable that they were amassed in a form of socio-political structure greater than that of an extended family as had been suggested by earlier explorers.

The year 1848 saw the beginning of emigrant and gold rush travel through Paiute country and, incidentally, the writing of one of the most complete diaries of a trip over the Spanish Trail. This was the journal of Orville C. Pratt, a lawyer of Rochester, New York, and Galena, Illinois, who traveled the route in the autumn of 1848.

Pratt had left Santa Fe on August 27th, bound for California. On September 26th, according to his diary, he camped "on the Sevier riv. after marching about 10 mi. ....This river is the recognized boundary of the Eutah country. Here commences the region occupied by the

48

Pah-Eutah Indians." This was a little south of present-day Salina, Utah, and in an area probably occupied by the San Pete and/or Fish Ute.

Continuing his description of the Paiute, Pratt remarked:

"They are said to be a poor, treacherous, and dangerous race of people. Stealing animals at night, & shooting them from the bluff & high points during the day, constitutes their principal mode of annoying the whites.

"Deer, elk, mountain sheep, and all sorts of game incident to the mountains, are here found in great abundance."

This initial statement by Pratt seems to indicate not only that the Paiutes were becoming more and more concerned with the defense of their territory against white incursions, but also that the food resources available to them were much greater than earlier travelers had indicated.

On the 30th of September, Pratt "camped at a fine spring in the first valley beyond or after leaving the Sevier." This was in Bear Valley, the trail having left the Sevier at Orton Junction, ten miles north of the present town of Panguitch. Here the emigrants "saw and caught two Pah Eutahs. . .They were much frightened at first, but soon became calm — These people seem greatly afraide [sic.] of the Spaniards, but towards the Americans they seem better disposed. . ."

Arriving in the vicinity of Little Salt Lake,

49

near present Parowan, on October 1st, Pratt noted that they were "in the center of...[an extensive valley where there]...was a fine lake of fish, with gravelly banks, and into which run 4 fine mountain streams & about 6 mi. apart." Here eight Paiutes stayed in the emigrants' camp overnight. The following day, on Coal Creek, Pratt wrote that "this valley is full of Pah-Utahs — and from what I have seen it seems the most desirable part of Mexico or California for agricultural purposes."

South of Cedar Valley, Pratt went thirty miles below the Vegas of Santa Clara "to the Piute cornfields on the Santa Clara river...The Piutes at this place are said to be the worst on the route. Bought some corn of them and made them some presents." This was just above Gunlock, Utah. The next day, while Pratt was continuing down the Santa Clara River, he remarked: "Two Piute Indians staid [sic.] with us last night, and behaved well — Their cornfields are frequently seen today on the river as we came along."

By October 10th, the Pratt party had reached the Muddy River, where they "found a large body of Indians. Piutes. From them we bought some green corn and beans." Apparently, the Paiute here were not so hostile as they had been only a few years before. Two days later, having made the long, dry march from the Muddy to Las Vegas, Pratt again saw Paiutes. In his journal

50

KAIBAB PAIUTE WOMEN out gathering seeds in 1872. The baskets they are carrying in their hands were used for beating seeds which were then placed in the conical burden baskets.

he noted: "Pah Eutahs here in great numbers but they run from us like wild deer."

The lawyer continued his diary with details of the trip across the Mohave Desert to Los Angeles, but his entry at Las Vegas contained the last reference to Indians along the route. Judging from his previous frequent mention of them, it is quite probable that he saw no others, or at least very few, west of Las Vegas. In all, however, this valuable report is quite definite in indicating that the country that lay along their route from the Sevier River at Salina, Utah, to Las Vegas, Nevada, was that of the Southern Paiute. The diary also gave more information about Paiute agriculture, especially considering that it was late in the fall of the year, than did earlier accounts. Certainly, along the Santa Clara, probably the Virgin, and the Muddy, a considerable amount of maize and bean farming was being carried on by the Indians.

In 1848, when thousands were on their way to the gold rush areas of California, most travelers went by way of the Overland Trail through northern Utah and Nevada. Only a few followed the Spanish Trail farther south. The diaries left by these fortune seekers almost invariably give details about the Southern Paiute similar to the records kept by Orville Pratt.

In reviewing the nature of contact between whites and Paiutes during the twenty year period from 1829 to 1849, two noticeable changes in Paiute culture and attitudes stand out. While their territory was nominally still under Spanish and Mexican control, these decades marked the beginning of Anglo-American exploration in at least portions of the Southern Paiute range. Beginning with the travels of James Ohio Pattie, contacts between Americans and Paiutes became increasingly unfriendly and in some instances overtly hostile. While the attitude of the Spanish explorers, so far as the records reveal, was friendly and sympathetic, Anglo-Americans tended to degrade the Indians either in their actual contacts with or in descriptions of them. It is unfortunate that we do not know more of the conditions of contact between Southern Paiute and the commercial Spanish and Mexican traders who followed Armijo beginning in 1831; these may have brought about increased stress and subsequent hostile attacks by both sides. While the Paiute attitudes can only be inferred, it may be suggested that the Indians were generally unaware of the import of these changes to their way of life. With what limited power they had, they either fought back or remained aloof from the Americans. On occasion, however, they harangued the explorers and emigrants or even came into their camps and traded with them. Paiutes along the Muddy tended to be more opposed to the American incursions than did those on the Santa Clara and to the north. This

53

opposition was largely opportunistic, marked by the occasional killing of livestock to augment their food supply or the ambush of a straggling traveler as a retaliatory measure. Elsewhere in the Paiute country away from the two main routes of European travel, and especially in the regions occupied by the Kaibab Paiute, the Indians had little if any contact with whites. Changes in the Indians' life ways, therefore, were much more rapid for Paiutes living along rivers such as the Muddy, the Virgin, and the Santa Clara. In spite of these numerous contacts on the trails, however, change and stress had but begun for the Paiute.

MORMON – PAIUTE CONTACT

The early 1850's saw the coming of Mormon settlers and missionaries to the Paiute. The first settlers to southern Utah were en route from the Great Salt Lake Valley in 1850 and within a year had established Cedar City. John D. Lee was appointed church recorder at this settlement and his letters to the *Deseret News,* together with the communications of others in the region, provide considerable information about Paiute culture change in the face of these more settled and permanent influences.

Lee, in a letter to the *Deseret News* on April 3, 1852, remarked about Paiute farming on the Santa Clara River: "On this stream we saw about 100 acres of land that had been cultivated by the Pintes Indians, principally in corn and squashes...This tribe is numerous, and have quite an idea of husbandry." That friction between the Mormons and the Paiutes soon developed is evident from another letter to the *Deseret News* written by John L. Smith from Parowan, Utah, on March 17, 1852. He said, in part:

"...We had a little trouble with the Pietes; a few killed or drove away two animals from the herd at bro. Johnson's; they were pursued, and two taken prisoners; they tried to get away and were shot. For a few days it caused hard feelings among some; they tried to retaliate, and injured one or two animals; they however, appear friendly, excepting two or three, but I think there is no danger to fear from them."

Paiute and Mormon relationships, however, frequently were peaceful and respectful. In June of the same year, for example, two Mormon settlers visited about 100 Paiute Indians camped around Panguitch Lake and "traded with them for their fish, giving them flour and bread." The Paiutes wanted gun powder from the Mormons but were refused.

On another trip, this time down the Virgin River, the same Mormons met more Paiutes and wrote:

"Here a number of Indians came to us...These Indians are very smart, quick and active, almost naked, with bright intellects...[they] showed us all the curiosities they could think of,

55

amongst the rest, a kind of weed that will quench thirst.

"We then got some Indian guides, who brought us to. . .Ash Creek, where we found a number of Indians raising grain. Their corn was waist high; squashes, beans, potatoes, &c., looked well. They had in cultivation some four or five acres; their wheat had got ripe and was cut. I looked around to see their tools, but could not see the first tool, only their hands, to dig their ditches, make dams, or anything else. The Piute chief made us a speech, showing their destitute situation, without clothes or food. Brother Lee told them we would learn them to work and raise breadstuff, make clothing, &c., at which they were well pleased, and wanted us to come soon and make a settlement among them. . ."

This letter is quite revealing. Apparently by the summer of 1852, the Mormons were in contact with certain local headmen, at least at Panguitch Lake and on the Virgin. New crops, potatoes and wheat, had been introduced to the Paiutes, probably by Mormons. And the latter were becoming interested in "improving" Indian farming techniques as well as in altering the natives' clothing. That at least some Southern Paiute desired even closer contact with the whites is indicated in their request for the establishment of settlements, a matter that John D. Lee also communicated to the *Deseret News* on August 7th:

"A few days ago we had a visit from the Toguer Captain, (or Black Chief), so called by the South Pah Eed Indians, with about thirty of his warriors. They were from the Santa Clara and Rio Virgin country, and wished to hold a council with me upon the subject of forming a settlement in their country."

But all relations were not so harmonious, especially with the Paiutes to the southwest on the Muddy River. Encamped there on November 17, 1852, on his way to a mission in China, was Hosea Stout. Here he wrote in his diary:

"Indians in large numbers geathered [*sic.*] around our company. One stole a lasso and was detected in an attempt to steel [*sic.*] a pair of boots & Burr Frost gave him a decent whaling, after which we drove them off not allowing them in camp any more."

Certainly, an analysis of these contact conditions must take into consideration variations in individual attitudes on the part of both white and Indian. For example, a view quite different from that of Stout was taken by William Adams, who wrote the *Deseret News* from Parowan on November 9th, 1852:

"I will say this much concerning the Indians — only for their labor, there would have been hundreds of bushels of produce lost, that could not have been saved by the white population. [There is no indication of a disaster here; probably the writer is referring to an over-abundant harvest.] I consider myself a common

57

hand, to work, but I must give up to some of the Piedes for quickness, and the Pahvantes (Indians) work considerable, but not so willingly as the Piedes or Pahutes. We have had from 20 to 40 lodges here through the summer and fall, averaging from one to two hundred natives."

Sporadic trouble did occur between the Paiute and non-Mormon emigrant trains moving through southern Utah in the 1850's. One such incident, reported in the *Deseret News,* is exemplary. In a letter to church President Brigham Young on January 24, 1854, John D. Lee wrote:

"There have been no outbreaks upon our settlement as yet, nor any depredations committed upon any of our animals, save two horses that were drove off west of the Iron Springs, by a couple of the uncivilized Piedes. The watchword was soon passed to us by some of the friendly natives...The Indians perceiving that they were closely pursued, shot the other horse seven times with arrows, then made their escape to the mountains.

"Reese's train passed this place about the 1st January. Reports have been brought by one of the Toquer Captain's sons...that three of his train were shot by the Indians on the first desert. Two of them they suppose to be mortally wounded; — and two horses stolen. I asked him why they committed the depredations; were not the company friendly? He replied that they were at first, and fed them the first night that they encamped on the Santa Clara, but that three Indians who lived on the Colorado

[Walapai?], that were afraid to come into camp, yet were hungry, in the night killed one of their horses to eat, but that they (the friendly Indians) knew nothing of the circumstances at the time, — In the morning a number of them went into camp, expecting a friendly reception. Directly they saw a man come into camp very much enraged; but what he said they knew not; but perceiving that evil was intended, they tried to make their retreat, when one of their number was shot dead on the ground, and three others wounded.

"This sad occurrence enraged the whole nation; they therefore cut across the mountains and waylaid the train and attacked them in a kanyon [sic.] on the Rio Virgin.

"This report has since been confirmed by the California Mail who narrowly escaped themselves from the Indians. They further said that Reese's men shot every Indian that came within reach of them; and that Reese had been robbed of 8000$ by his own company; and that about one half of his animals and wagons were left scattered on the desert; and that Reese himself had gone ahead for supplies for his company."

And what did Mr. Enoch Reese have to say of this incident? On February 6, 1854, he, too, wrote to Brigham Young giving his version of the affair:

"From Utah Valley, all things went along well until we got to the Santa Clara. Here we had a fuss with the Indians, tho' they were not to blame in the affair. During the afternoon, five Indians with their chief, came to the train as it

59

was moving down the Santa Clara, and wished to know if they could come to our train in the evening. We told them they could, and we would give them some flour. They then left well satisfied.

"While this agreement was making, a company of packers, who were just ahead, came across some Indians in the road and fired on them, killing one, tho' they deny killing any; still I think it can be proved that they killed one. When this took place, the chief we had conversed with came back to the train and said, the packers had killed one of his men, and they would now try to kill the whites, and he could not restrain them but felt sorry that any trouble had taken place.

"There was another company traveling with us, a man named Wilson being their captain; they were the hindmost wagons; the Indians fell upon this company, wounding three — one of them quite severely, the others slightly. This created quite an excitement, and we sent back and brought all up.

"I expressed my indignation at the course of some who were traveling with us, and told them if they could not travel without killing the Indians, we would divide the train. . ."

It is not possible, of course, to ascertain all activities of the parties involved in this matter. But, if "Indians who lived on the Colorado" did kill a horse as was reported to Lee, it is probable that they were either some Uinkarets Paiute from south of the Virgin River, or some Walapai from across the Colorado, visiting in Toquer's "band." The visitors, at any rate, probably had had little if any previous contact with Anglo-Americans; they were apprehensive about approaching the camp of the wagon train although the possibility of obtaining a horse for food must have enticed them. The role of the "company of packers" remains in doubt; there is no additional record of them. It seems quite probable, however, that some "Americans," as Mormons often referred to non-Mormons, felt that their only course of action was to fire upon the Indians as retribution for the killing of the horse.

Other attacks, by the Paiute and the Ute, continued in Utah, perhaps the best known being the ambush of Captain Gunnison by Pahvant Utes on the Sevier River north of Paiute territory.

Lieutenant Sylvester Mowry, who was in Utah in 1855 as a member of a force investigating the Gunnison massacre, believed that the Mormons had incited the Indians to riot. Of the Southern Paiute, Mowry wrote:

"During my march, I found on the Santa Clara, Virgin, Muddy, and Vegas Rivers several hundred warriors who had undergone [this] tutelage. In each tribe two or more Mormon Missionaries were found, whose sole object was to impress upon the Indians the belief in the inferiority and hostility of the Americans, and the superiority and friendship of the Mormons. The Indians on the Santa Clara have been supplied with arms and ammunition to a great extent. More than seventy were counted in and around my camp, all armed with good rifles. Two years ago they were armed with nothing but bows and arrows of the poorest description."

Although Mowry perhaps exaggerated the Mormon influence, his account does indicate how rapidly the Paiute acquired firearms after Mormon colonization began.

Mormon policy involved more than the establishment of settlements among the Paiute. While Brigham Young took the attitude that "It is better to feed them than to fight them," there was also a very strong feeling that Mormon missionaries had a duty to "save" the Indians. John D. Lee and others had preached to the Paiute almost as soon as they arrived in southern Utah, but it was not until October of 1853 that the first "Mission to the Indians Inhabiting the Southern Parts of the Territory of Utah" was organized. This mission, which left Salt Lake city on April 14, 1854, was directed by Rufus C. Allen until August of 1857 when Jacob Hamblin was placed in charge. Thomas D. Brown was the recorder, and it is essentially his journal, containing almost daily records from April 14, 1854, to May 20, 1855, that provides the detailed record of Mormon activities among the Southern Paiute during this period.

While individual Mormons held varying

THE SUMMER CAMP OF CHUARUMPEAK, chief of the Kaibab Paiutes, south of Kanab, in 1872. The chief is the man in the beaded buckskin shirt.

attitudes about the Indians, the most common belief was that they were "savages" to be taught "civilized" ways. As William Adams wrote in his autobiography in 1853: "Jacob Hamblin and others were missionaries to the Indians in Utah, civilizing and teaching them to work, trying to raise them up from their low filthy conditions and be self sustaining." And Thomas Brown, writing to the *Desert News* from Harmony, Utah, on May 19, 1854, after remarking upon some Mormon irrigated fields, said that this work had been done so that:

"We shall be enabled to feed the Indians [Paiutes], keep them around us, learn their language, and do them good. We purpose [*sic.*] establishing a school for the Indian youth. . .We are much in want of old clothing, especially shirts, to help cover the nakedness of the Indians, especially of the women."

This was not to be an attempt at rapid assimilation, however. After the mission had arrived at Harmony, south of Cedar City, on Sunday, May 14, 1854, Brother Groves spoke to the assembly saying: "Take not their wild habits and liberty from them at once, but by degrees, and help them to farm, but let them labor for their food." And Brother Lott remarked: "We must treat them like children, by degrees, to quit their savage customs."

While the missionaries labored at Harmony, preparing fields for the Paiute to farm, Brigham

64

Young arrived on May 19th with more explicit instructions:

"You are sent [he said] not to farm, build nice houses and fence fine fields, not to help white men, but to save the red ones, learn their language, and you can do this more effectively by living among them...go with them where they go, live with them and when they rest let them live with you, feed them clothe them, and teach them as you can...[and] not many generations shall pass away till they become a white and delightsome people..."

This, as was the case with Christian missionaries working among Indians elsewhere in the United States, set the tone for most future relations between the Mormons and the Southern Paiute.

Recorder Brown's journal also contains some pertinent anthropological information about the Paiute in the 1850's. In early June, 1854, for example, he noted the Indians' burial customs, saying: "When they inter a body they bury all with it, the blanket, or rabbit skin mantilla, bows and arrows, or gun if they have one"; he added that the mother of a dead child refused their entreaties to bury it in a coffin "after our fashion."

Brown also provided a description of Toquer's camp along Ash Creek:

"the Chief Toquer's Wickeups [houses] Composed of long branches of willows, cotton-wood and stalks of corn, 3 of them — the willows stuck in the ground slantingly so that they meet at the top, the leaves of these and a neighboring ash tree was all the shelter from wind or rain. . .They have small stripes [*sic.*] of corn, squash, and potatoes, &c., all scratched in with their hands, for miles along Ash Creek and seem very industrious. We went over to their Wicke-ups after our supper and found their women grinding seeds by the light of the moon, and boiling a large potful of porridge — in a conical shaped dish made from clay and sand thin and hard. This mass seemed of a darkish grey color with like chunks of bacon in it. We tasted the flour which the women were making from the seeds of grass — by rubbing them between two rocks. It tasted much like buckwheat flour or bean meal. What we fancied to be pieces of bacon, I have been told were bunches of matted ants. . .this porridge the female stirred with a large spoon or ladle, like the water gourds. . . made from the horn of a mountain sheep; with this the mess was divided on wicker baskets, flat, in the shape of flat wood turned dishes, about 1 quart to each — the elder served first — this was soon cleaned out by bending the forefinger of the right hand inwards around the point of the tumb for a spoon — the same dish handed back and filled and passed around. They supped this up greedily, and with the head of a roasted porcupine, brains and bones, added to an entire roasted sand lark, seemed, added to what we gave them — to about satisfy."

Of similar interest to this description of a Paiute meal is Brown's record of a curing ceremony by a medicine man or shaman. Just a few miles up

66

the Santa Clara River from the Indian camp he commented upon above, the missionaries came to another settlement where they baptized 11 Paiute men. He saw there a healing rite which he described as follows:

". . .medicine man came to-day, and after giving the sick woman, some hot water to drink, but no herbs in it, begain to sing, 'Nani, nani, nani, Nani, nani,' &c., varying the sound. . .first loud then falling by degrees, then beginning aloud again, this he continued, till, I suppose, having invoked the healing spirit long enough he would get to his knees, then roll over to his back would draw himself close up the patient, and with closed eyes, still singing, lift up his hands so as to receive her, she would fall across him and he placing his arms around her and near the sore shoulder, would begin to press her breast, would crawl out when breath seemed almost gone to him, would spit out some nasty green stuff, expectorated from his own lungs, or chest, would again begin a new murmuring song 'Ha-a-a-a Ha-a-a-a Hum-m-m-m,' &c., would continue again for half an hour till he would again fall on his back, again receive her into his arms crosswise — again suck till he would expectorate one of his dark green stones — about the size of a bean, this he would carry off, crawling in a stooping posture some 20 yards and hide it among the brushes or in the earth, buying the disease or evil spirit. These stones they carry in their medicine bags — and I doubt not resurrect all they bury, at their own convenience, for I suppose they esteem these stones sacred; then he returned and would begin singing, continue again in the same way till after another pressure and suction — a white stone would be expectorated and burried [*sic.*], this continued for two hours, crawling off once on his hands and knees and once sucking the shoulder and pressing the breast."

This is the best account available of the ministrations of a Southern Paiute shaman at such an early period and it agrees well with similar information gathered by professional ethnologists working with these Indians much later. Indeed, curing by sucking on the afflicted portion of the patient's body was typical for many tribes in the American West.

In sum, Brown's notes present a reasonably full picture of Paiute camps and camp life. Agricultural practices, gathering techniques, food preparation, wikiup construction, shamanism, death customs, and even, to a lesser degree, socio-political organization are described in more detail than in any previous account. From an analysis of these behavioral patterns it is obvious that changes in Paiute life were taking place at different rates depending upon the particular aspect of culture, individual personalities, and degree of sustained contact. In 1854, at least among the Southern Paiute living in southwestern Utah along major streams, the pre-contact traits embodied in the native religion, social structure, agricultural and gathering techniques, food preparation, architecture, and

Smithsonian Institution National Anthropological Archieves, Neg. No. 1623
A KAIBAB PAIUTE ROUND DANCE in 1872. Most of the participants are wearing typical rabbit fur robes for winter weather protection.

material equipment (with a few exceptions such as the addition of certain articles of European clothing and iron tipped arrows) remained essentially as it had been before the white man came. Some domestic plants, such as potatoes, wheat, and melons had been introduced to them; efforts were being made to spur the Indians to greater agricultural industriousness; some individuals, particularly those in proximity to the settlements, were working for the Mormons and had, at least nominally, accepted their faith. It is probable, also, that the Mormons were affecting Paiute political patterns by appointing native leaders who were allied with them. Distant from these Mormon villages, Paiutes living to the south in the Uinkarets Mountains or on the Kaibab Plateau presumably were but little affected. The Mormons as yet had no direct contact with them.

In reviewing the historic observations made of Southern Paiutes during the two decades from 1860 to 1880, it is clear that similar conditions continued. Some Paiute continued to adopt the white man's ways while some remained hostile. Almost all of whom we have any record attempted to maintain as much of their native way of life as possible. Some Shivwits Paiute from the vicinity of present St. George, Utah, even sought "asylum" with the Walapai and Havasupai across the Colorado River in the hope of avoiding Mormon efforts to change them.

By this time, more definite changes in native political structure took place with the emergence of "bands", usually named after some locality in their particular territory, and under the leadership of "chiefs." These groupings, however, were only partly military, probably in an attempt to discourage further Anglo-American incursions. This was to no avail, and white men continued to pass through and settle on the range of the Southern Paiute.

The settlement of Kanab, Utah, in the territory of the Kaibab band of Southern Paiute was established in the spring of 1864, and stock ranches were soon located nearby at places such as Pipe Springs, Moccasin Springs, and Short Creek. Soon another threat to the Paiutes made itself known. Navajo Indians, probably by 1865 and certainly no later than 1870, had crossed the Colorado River and were "marauding the southern parts of Utah" according to Ammon Tenney, one of Jacob Hamblin's assistants. On the 18th of December, 1865, Indians attacked the settlement at Kanab for the purpose of stealing horses belonging both to the settlers and to the Paiutes. "A few of the brethren and about 25 Piedes followed the thieving Indians toward the Pahreach [Paria River], but did not succeed in recovering the stock."

Into this milieu in the summer of 1869 came Major John Wesley Powell and his associates, bent upon topographic exploration, but with a

71

developing concern for Indian affairs.

On Powell's first trip down the Colorado River through the Grand Canyon he saw what must have been a Uinkarets Paiute garden near the mouth of either Whitmore Wash or Parashont Canyon. There were no Indians there but Powell and his men helped themselves to the corn and squash that were ripe. Several days farther down the river, at the western end of Grand Canyon, Powell came upon a Paiute encampment consisting of temporary structues of boughs. He talked with a man, dressed only in a hat, and with a woman wearing but a string of beads.

A year later, in September of 1870, Powell, with the help of the missionary Jacob Hamblin, was in the isolated Arizona "Strip" country just north of Grand Canyon and south of the Mormon settlements of St. George and Kanab. He had met and talked with "Chu-ar-um-peak, the chief of the Kai-vav-its" about two matters important to him: the fate of three of his men who had left his 1869 river party in an attempt to climb out of the Canyon through Paiute territory, and about land routes into the Canyon by means of which he could supply future river explorations. Near Mount Trumbull, on September 17, 1870, Paiute guides apologetically told Powell of the killing of the three men a year previous. They had thought the explorers were part of a group of white men who had earlier molested some Paiute women and could not believe that, instead, they had actually journeyed by boat down the Colorado River.

Powell's journals for this period would indicate that the Kaibab and adjoining bands of Southern Paiute in this isolated region north of Grand Canyon were still living under essentially native conditions. At the same time, however, Jacob Hamblin seemed concerned about Paiute subsistence. In a letter to Major Powell that Hamblin wrote from Kanab on December 20, 1870, the Mormon "peacemaker" noted that:

"I have not yet had any goods for the benefit of the Kiabab [sic.] Indians. I would like to get a few for them if I could. I heard that the Supt. of Indian Affairs in Salt Lake City had some goods for the Southern Utah Indians, expecting they would be used in a way to favor your business next season."

Hamblin apparently thought that by so couching his appeal to Powell, the Major would be able to intercede with the Utah Indian agent. It is also an indication of the continuing efforts on the part of the Mormon missionaries to introduce new things to the Paiute. Indeed, some Kaibab Paiute by this time had moved to settle near Mormon towns. In a *Deseret News* article on April 21, 1871, entitled "The Kanab Region," it was reported that "the Indians in the immediate vicinity of Kanab settlements are peaceable and industrious."

This was to do more to change the native way of life of the Kaibab than any previous contact. In the fall of the same year, Major Powell commented upon the condition of the Paiutes near the settlements. He said:

"The Pah-Utes prowl about, begging, doing odd jobs, and selling Indian trinkets. Short in stature, half starved, scantily-clothed, they present a pitiful, abject appearance. The squaws transport their progeny in Konunkwas — willow baby-baskets, covered with buckskin."

In April, 1872, Hamblin's long-awaited shipment of goods for the Paiutes finally arrived. He and Major Powell arranged a meeting with the Indians at Washington, a few miles east of St. George. Paiute from the Shivwits, Santa Clara, and Kaibab districts were present, as were some of Powell's men, one of whom recounted the affair:

"The Sheviwets were arranged in a circle seated on the ground, each band with its chief, of whom there were 3...[Goods distributed included]...blankets, shirts, cotton cloth, drill, ...blue flannel, butcher knives, some hoes, axes and shovels. About 11 A.M. the natives became very hungry and we gave them some flour and meat, and waited until they had eaten, when the young men gave us a dance, then we finished the distribution. Old Moqueop, an old Sheviwit, made a speech telling them that they must be good 'wano' Indians or the Americans would make them no more presents. Then Pa-Ute

CHUARUMPEAK WATCHING A GAMBLING GAME. The object was to guess which hand of one's opponent held a bone with a wrapping of buckskin. The sticks in the ground are counters.

Frank [Chuarumpeak, the Kaibab band leader] talked awhile and the conference closed. He is a good speaker, is a young man and is trying to become chief of all the tribes in southern Utah. . .Counted while they were at dinner 106 Indians, mostly men; but few women or children present. Think government can be induced to establish an agency for them. . .Jacob Hamblin will try to persuade them to farm some."

Analysis of this account indicates some changes in Southern Paiute leadership patterns at this time as well as economic disorganization resulting from stresses of the immediate past. If the description is correct in assessing the motives of Chuarumpeak, the Kaibab leader, it is the earliest documentation relative to an effort at leadership consolidation among the several Paiute groups of southern Utah. Jacob Hamblin's efforts to persuade the assembled Paiute "to farm some," in light of the documentation that it was among Paiutes from these same groups where agriculture was most consistently carried on earlier, would seem to indicate that many of them had abandoned farming as a means of subsistence. This could have occurred only in the decade of two prior to the 1872 meeting, probably the result of a somewhat paternalistic attitude of the dominant society in its efforts to change the Indians.

As one might expect, the now prolonged contact that the Paiutes had with white men brought about the introduction of diseases new

MAJOR POWELL AND JACOB HAMBLIN meet with Kaibab Paiutes in 1872. Of the two white men present, Powell is nearest the camera.

to the Indians. One of Powell's photographers, Beaman, on a trip south of Kanah, camped in a small valley. This valley, he reported:

"bears the ominous title of 'The Valley of Death'; this from the fact that at one time it was the camping-ground of a tribe of the Pah-Utes, where, the measles breaking out among them, a hundred deaths occurred in a very few days. The place was abandoned, and thereafter avoided by the Indians, unless forced to visit it by a pressing need of water."

This, however, is one of the few documents relating to epidemics among the Paiute aside from Edward Palmer's brief reference to a smallpox epidemic before 1877.

The United States Bureau of Indian Affairs began to take more interest in conditions among the Southern Paiute in the 1870's. A Paiute reservation had been established at Moapa, Nevada, in 1873 and the Bureau sent Major Powell and Major G. W. Ingalls, as a special Bureau of Indian Affairs commission, to investigate Indian conditions and complaints by Anglo-Americans that they were "preparing to commence a war of extermination against the whites," a fear that proved groundless. Of the Paiutes, they wrote:

"The Pai-Utes inhabit Southern Itah, Southern Nevada, Northern Arizona, and South-eastern California.

"There is a small tribe in the vicinity of

78

Beaver, and another at Parowan. . .A third tribe is. . .found. . .in the vicinity of Cedar."

They also listed a tribe of Paiute in Long Valley consisting of about 125 persons, one in Kanab Valley of about 107, a few on the Paria River, and about 47 on the "eastern" side of the Colorado. The Uinkarets numbered about 60 and the Shivwits about 180 according to their estimates. Others were scattered "in small tribes, and hold allegiance to many petty chiefs." The commissioners described the Paiute as cultivators, gatherers and beggars, and a serious burden to the settlers. They reported that the Indians understood that they could no longer economically sustain themselves in an aboriginal fashion and that:

"They fully understand that the settlement of the country by white men is inevitable. . .Their hunting-grounds have been spoiled, their favorite valleys are occupied by white men, and they are compelled to scatter in small bands in order to obtain subsistence."

In noting that each band wanted its own reservation, Powell and Ingalls first suggested removing them from the country and, later, to either the Muddy (Moapa) Reservation or to the Uintah Ute Reservation in northern Utah. An attempt at the latter proved unsuccessful, but Powell and Ingalls justified their stand on the Moapa by remarking that there was good land and plenty of water, but no hunting lands. They argued that all Southern Paiute and Chemehuevi be collected on the Moapa reserve and taught how to farm. This, of course, was an attitude typical of all government officials who attempted to settle Indians on reserves all over the West at this time. Removal of Anglo-American settlers who already occupied the best lands of the Moapa Reservation also was stipulated. In conclusion, Powell and Ingalls reported to the Commissioner of Indian Affairs:

"The country inhabited by these Indians [Southern Paiute] no longer affords game in sufficient quantities worthy to be mentioned as part of their subsistence. A very few deer and mountain-sheep are killed, and a greater number of rabbits. The principal part of their food is obtained by gathering seeds and digging roots. All of the tribes cultivate the soil to a limited extent, raising wheat, corn, beans, melons, and squashes. Some food and the greater part of their clothing is obtained by begging, the skins of such animals as they kill being entirely inadequate to their wants for this purpose."

Powell had indicated that the Southern Paiute had agreed to the move to the Moapa Reservation and he requested from the Bureau the sum of $32,000 to extinguish the rights of about 40 white settlers within its confines.

Commenting upon the conditions of Great Basin Indians in general, it was Powell's opinion that the "Indians are begging for land. They say,

80

fix it so that we can stay here, and so white men can not take this land from us and we can get a living for ourselves." The Major even went so far as to suggest that the government say to the Indians: "'We will secure you land, build you houses, and give you a cow' and the greater number of Indians will go" to the reserves.

Such statements are but another reflection of the stress conditions under which the Southern Paiute were operating in the 1870's. They apparently were willing to agree to Powell's stipulations of reservation life in exchange for a secure land base free from further white encroachments so long as it was somewhere within their former territory.

Thus was the stage set upon which the Southern Paiute lost much of their native territory — territory for which they were not compensated for almost one hundred years. As it turned out, not all the Paiute went to Moapa because within a few decades other reservations were established for them.

Mormon missionary activities continued among the Paiute. In the spring of 1875, "about 200 Shebit [Shivwits] Indians" were baptized near St. George. It appears, according to the sources of the time, that shamanistic visions were responsible for Paiute willingness to be converted or at least "to carry out any suggestions that the Saints might make." Such compliance, however, was probably simply another attempt by the Paiute to relieve the stress conditions confronting them.

In 1878, Major Ingalls was in St. George, still attempting to effect the removal of the Paiutes to the Moapa Reservation. Such segregation, however, was not to happen. The Shivwits Reservation near Santa Clara was established in 1891 and added to in 1916 until it comprised a total of 26,800 acres, of which about 72 acres were tillable. By 1900 about 100 Kaibab Paiute had concentrated around Moccasin Spring southwest of Kanab and a 12 by 18 mile reserve was established for them there in 1907; this was extended by executive order in 1913 and again in 1917.

By the first decade of the twentieth century, the historic transculturation of the Southern Paiute was virtually complete. Frederick Dellenbaugh, one of Powell's boatmen and artist on the 2nd Colorado River Expedition in 1871, returned to Kanab 32 years later. He had known the Kaibab Paiute quite well in the 70's and, now, in 1903, had brought with him some trinkets to trade with them. These included four pairs of scissors and two looking glasses. But, Dellenbaugh sold them to Hamblin's store since, in his words:

"I had no time to go to their camp, and from what I hear, imagine they make very few articles now of any kind. They cannot get buckskin and

MORMONS BAPTIZING Southern Paiute near St. George, Utah. 1875.

their whole method of living has changed, though they still occupy rickety wicky-ups." Any semblance of native, aboriginal Southern Paiute life was a thing of the past.

RECENT HISTORY AND THE PRESENT

During the first half of the twentieth century, the Kaibab and other bands of Southern Paiute lived in comparative obscurity. At least, they were little known beyond the immediate areas of their reservations. In addition to the Moapa, Shivwits, and Kaibab reserves, lands were set aside for them at Las Vegas, Nevada, and at Indian Peak and Koosharem, Utah. Other Southern Paiute continued to live on the outskirts of Mormon towns such as Cedar City and Richfield, also in Utah. If their obscurity was relative, their poverty verged on the absolute. At Moapa and Shivwits they continued to farm in a minimum fashion. Elsewhere, they were almost totally dependent upon the Bureau of Indian Affairs and assistance from the Mormons. As a result, more and more Paiutes expressed belief in the doctrines of the Church of Jesus Christ of Latter Day Saints. Part of this largesse, as far as the Kaibab Paiutes were concerned, consisted of an agreement whereby the Indians were given one-third of the water from Moccasin Spring, a source of water that the Paiutes had exclusively used for centuries. It will be remembered that the Mormons had established a settlement at this

84

Photograph by Robert C. Euler

A YOUNG SOUTHERN PAIUTE GIRL on the Shivwits Reservation holding two cradle boards made by her grandmother.

spring in the 1860's. Much later, it was reported by Dr. E. A. Farrow, the Superientendent of the Kaibab Reservation from 1917 to 1926, that the Indians "were driven out by white settlers and became nomadic, making their base in and around Kanab." Some time after that, but before the Reservation was established in 1907, through the offices of the Mormon Church in Kanab, there was obtained "a grant from the squatters at Moccasin Spring of one-third of the flow of the spring and they were allowed to farm a small tract of land nearby, watering it from the spring."

With the establishment of the reservation, a day school for the Indians and some other buildings were constructed about two miles from the spring. A pipe line to carry the Indians' share of the water was also installed to the school.

Farrow reported that the Kaibab population at that time and immediately after fluctuated around 100.

Apparently, according to Farrow's report, there was also a public school at Moccasin Spring for the white children. "Sentiment on the part of the whites against the admission of these [Indian] children into the public school at Moccasin", he said, "has made it necessary to maintain the day school" at least until 1930. Fortunately, these animosities have long since passed.

The Bureau of Indian Affairs issued cattle to the Kaibab at the time their reservation was established. This was in the hope that the Indians would turn more to animal husbandry than to farming since water for agricultural purposes was scarce. While a good herd was built up, this soon was disseminated. In 1916, another herd was purchased and by 1930 sufficient Indians had become involved in cattle raising that Farrow termed the project successful. In fact, in a somewhat predictive mood, Farrow wrote that:

"The Indians at first doubtful became enthusiastic and even the young boys are getting into the cattle business. The outlook of these Indians is as good as that of their white neighbors and their knowledge of the cattle business gleaned from watching the growth and development of the tribal herd will enable most of them to be self-supporting without the need of searching for labor on the outside as they have been doing, and still do."

Speaking about the health of the Kaibab Paiute, Farrow, who as the physician to the tribe should have been in a good position to know, indicated that they were more free from epidemics than were the neighboring Anglo-Americans; a few cases of tuberculosis were all he noted.

For the next twenty years, through the economic depression of the 1930's and the war of the 1940's, the Kaibab Paiute merely existed.

Photograph by Robert C. Euler

CLEAN AIR AND BLUE SKIES are some of the rewards to one fortunate enough to stand on this spot — the location of the new tribal office of the Kaibab Paiute — the north rim of the Grand Canyon 50 miles to the South is clearly seen.

Men worked for wages occasionally but for most of the time they were dependent upon the charity of the dominant society.

Then, at mid-century, two events took place — events that were destined ultimately to provide them with the potential for economic well-being that had been denied them virtually since the coming of the white men.

First of all, they established their official constitution and bylaws under the terms of the Wheeler-Howard or the Indian Reorganization Act. While this act was passed by Congress in 1934, the Kaibab people did not act upon it until 1951. The wording, especially that of the preamble, almost seems to have come intact from the days of Powell and Ingalls. It says that the Paiute established their constitution "in order to show our gratefulness to Almighty God, and to improve ourselves in the art of civilization. . ." Nonetheless, it gave to these impoverished people a more secure land base and at least some measure of self-determination of their affairs through the establishment of a duly elected tribal council. Although the import of this constitution may have been lost upon some at the time, it was to prove an important legal step for the future.

About the same time, the Kaibab Paiute along with several other Southern Paiute groups, acting under the provisions of the Indian Claims Act passed by Congress in 1946, filed suit against the United States Government claiming restitution payment for all their aboriginal lands that had been wrongfully taken from them by the Government or agents thereof. Their case dragged on and, ultimately, was rather bitterly fought before the Indian Claims Commission in 1956. Decision as to its outcome was also slow in coming, but finally they won it and received a judgment in 1970.

Meanwhile, most of the other Southern Paiute bands had petitioned to have their Federal trusteeship terminated. They wanted to be cut free from major ties with the Government and this request was granted in 1957. Almost immediately, most of their reservation lands were sold or transferred to other ownership and, while these bands, also, will realize the benefits from their land claims settlements, their land base, in most instances, is no longer secure.

The Kaibab Paiute, with a reservation of 120,413 acres, a population of 136, and a land claim settlement of slightly over one million dollars, are on the threshold of better times at last.

Today, some fourteen families, comprising 62 people, live in the small settlement of Kaibab, two miles from Moccasin Spring. The remaining 74 individuals live nearby. While a few still live in small, frame houses, ten other families reside in attractive and recently completed "self help" concrete block structures. The main roads are paved, thus easing transportation problems especially in the snowy winter months. A spacious tribal administrative building was officially dedicated on June 2nd, 1970, providing adequate offices and meeting facilities for the tribal council and other employees.

Reservation lands are not yet used to their full economic potential. Until recently, approximately 10,000 acres of grazing land were leased to non-Indian ranchers but the remainder was not in any type of production.

There are two private enclaves within the Kaibab Reservation boundaries. One of these, 400 acres, comprises the Mormon settlement of Moccasin. The other tract, of 40 acres, is the National Park Service facility of Pipe Springs National Monument, an early Mormon "fort" around a small spring.

The Kaibab Paiutes receive medical and dental care through contract services with physicians and dentists in nearby communities, a program financed by the United States Public Health Service. There is also a resident P.H.S. community health worker on the reservation.

Paiute children — and of the total population of 136, forty-four are under the age of 16 — attend a one room public school in Moccasin. From the 6th grade through high school, however, they are bussed to Fredonia, twelve miles to the east. Approximately 10 Paiute children are now in high school and four others are attending college. Individual income producing opportunities on the reservation are few. The tribal chairman is the only salaried employee of the tribe. Three other Indians are employed by the Public Health Service, the Bureau of Indian Affairs, and the Indian Development District of Arizona. The National Park Service occasionally employs one Indian as a maintenance person. Beyond that, other Indians, mostly men, obtain part-time work on nearby white owned cattle ranches.

With the availability of land claims funds, some of the chronic under-employment may be alleviated at least temporarily. The Kaibab Tribal Council has allocated 15% of the total claim payment to per capita distribution. This amounts to slightly over $1,000 per individual. An additional 15% has been budgeted for a "family plan." These funds are distributed by the council to enable families to pay off past debts, obtain household furnishings, and other immediate family needs. Both of these budgeted items are being released to the Paiute at the present time. The remaining 70% of the land claim monies are being budgeted as follows: Education, 10%; Tribal Enterprises, 35%; Community Development, 15%; and Administration, 10%. None of these funds has as yet been expended.

94

In sum, when one looks back upon the past tribulations of the Paiutes as they have attempted to adjust to the inroads and demands of the dominant society, one is amazed that they have been able to survive as a viable tribal group. Yet, with perseverance and with a better understanding of the white man than the whites have of them, they have not only managed to cling to some of their land but have also built a much more secure position for themselves in the larger society of Arizona.

THE FUTURE

All of this is not to say that the future of the Kaibab Paiute is totally unclouded. Since on-reservation employment opportunities are not good, and since most of the people, including the younger members of the tribe, want to remain there, it is imperative that a more stable economic base be established.

With the portions of the land claims payments allocated for Tribal Enterprise and Community Development some plans for this are under consideration. The tribe wants to let its grazing lands renew themselves for a few years and then stock them with their own cattle. It would like to put approximately 10,000 acres into agriculture, if, and it is a big if, adequate water supplies can be developed. The Paiutes still retain their rights to one-third of the Moccasin Spring water, but this is not sufficient for large scale farming operations.

Since thousands of tourists visit Pipe Springs National Monument each year and still more spend time at both Zion and Bryce Canyon National Parks in the vicinity, the tribe would like to further develop its own tourist potential. Plans for an attractive cultural center, arts and crafts shop, restaurant, and camp ground adjoining the present tribal building are on the drawing board. The beautiful scenery of the northern part of the reservation and the limited hunting potential, however, are not enough to attract large numbers of visitors. Tribal leaders would very much like to develop the outstanding archaeological potential on their lands. Within a hundred yards of the tribal administrative center is a large, unexcavated prehistoric Pueblo ruin that was occupied some time around A.D. 1100. Professional archaeologists from Prescott College have estimated that it would cost approximately $50,000 to excavate and stabilize this large E shaped structure. The tribe does not have such funds available and the acquisition of them from outside sources is a prime need. With that prehistoric ruin excavated and properly interpreted by trained Paiute rangers, a most worthwhile historical picture of the area could be presented to summer visitors. The ruin would tell the story of the early human occupation

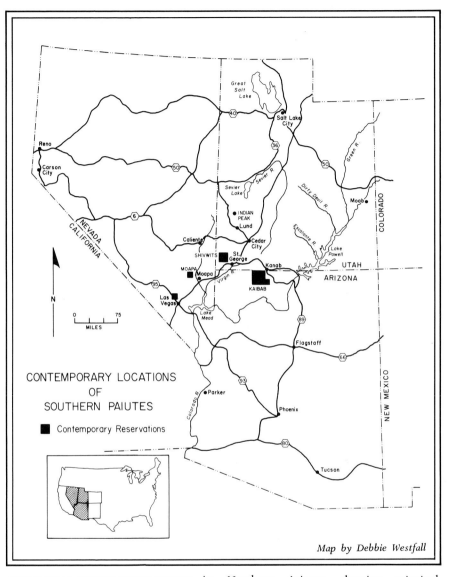

THE KAIBAB PAIUTE RESERVATION in Northern Arizona showing principal travel routes.

there. The Mormon "fort" at Pipe Springs, also within a hundred yards of the prehistoric site, would provide the background for Mormon settlement, and a tribal museum in the cultural center could explain the history and culture of the Southern Paiutes. There is an all-weather paved road, Arizona state highway 389, leading west from Fredonia to the tribal headquarters on the reservation 12 miles distant. This highway continues into southern Utah and provides an easy and scenic route to Zion Canyon National Park as well as to the access road to Grand Canyon National Monument.

Additional support for education of Paiute youth is also needed. While some funds are available from the Bureau of Indian Affairs for college scholarships, the educational item in the land claims budget should provide more. More than just money is needed, however. An incentive for young Paiute men and women to complete a higher education, or even, in some cases, high school, is still lacking. The present tribal leadership is excellent, but younger people who will be needed by the tribe in the future need to be trained for these roles.

With continued strong leaders and with the assistance of various state and government agencies, especially the economically oriented Indian Development District of Arizona, the future of the Kaibab looks good. What could be added to these ingredients, however, is a more realistic awareness of the Paiute by white people in surrounding communities and , indeed, in the state of Arizona and Utah as a whole. And that awareness must include the very important factor that the Paiutes are perfectly capable of making their own decisions about their future and, at long last, should be permitted to put them into operation without pressure from the dominant society.

SUGGESTED READINGS

Many of the historical sources used in the text are out of print and are available only in major libraries. This is one reason why so many lengthy direct quotations were included. However, other accurate accounts of the Southern Paiute are readily obtainable. Some of the best are:

ALTER, J. CECIL. "The Mormons and the Indians." *Utah Historical Quarterly*, Vol. 12. Salt Lake City, 1944.

This is an introductory sketch outlining Mormon relations with the Indians of Utah, including the Southern Paiute.

BOLTON, HERBERT E. "Pageant in the Wilderness. The Story of the Escalante Expedition to the Interior Basin, 1776, including the Diary and Itinerary of Father Escalante." *Utah Historical Quarterly*, Vol. 18. Salt Lake City, 1950.

The facinating and highly readable account of the first European exploration of Southern Paiute territory.

BROOKS, JUANITA. "Indian Relations on the Mormon Frontier." *Utah Historical Quarterly*, Vol. 12. Salt Lake City, 1944.

An account by one of the foremost of

Mormon historians; especially valuable for southern Utah history.

CLELAND, ROBERT GLASS AND JUANITA BROOKS (EDITORS). *A Mormon Chronicle: The Diaries of John D. Lee, 1848-1876.* San Marino, California: The Huntington Library, 1955.

The annotated journals of this important Utah pioneer including his missionary efforts among the Paiute, the establishment of his ferry across the Colorado, and his efforts to avoid implication in the Mountain Meadows Massacre.

DELLENBAUGH, FREDERICK S. *A Canyon Voyage, The Narrative of the Second Powell Expedition down the Green-Colorado River from Wyoming and the Explorations on Land in the Years 1871-1872.* New Haven: Yale University Press, 1926.

Yale University has recently released a paperback edition of Dellenbaugh's narrative which not only recounts his harrowing river trip through Grand Canyon, but also his experiences with the Kaibab Paiute.

EULER, ROBERT C. "Southern Paiute Archaeology." *American Antiquity,* Volume 29, 1964.

A somewhat technical report of the pre-history of the Southern Paiute.

EULER, ROBERT C. *Southern Paiute Ethnohistory.* University of Utah Anthropological Papers, Number 78. Salt Lake City: 1966. A definitive monograph of the cultural history of these Indians from 1776 to 1900.

HAFEN, LEROY R. AND ANN W. HAFEN. *Journals of Forty-Niners, Salt Lake to Los Angeles.* Glendale, California: Arthur H. Clark Co., 1954. Detailed description of all the major travels over the Old Spanish Trail during the Gold Rush Days.

HAFEN, LEROY R. AND ANN W. HAFEN. *Old Spanish Trail: Santa Fè to Los Angeles.* Glendale, California: Arthur H. Clark Co., 1954. An analysis of Spanish, Mexican, and American trips on this route through Paiute country from 1776 on.

KELLY, ISABEL T. "Southern Paiute Bands." *American Anthropologist,* Volume 36, 1934. The political composition and location of the several bands of Southern Paiute, including the Kaibab.

KELLY, ISABEL T. *Southern Paiute Ethnography.* University of Utah Anthropological Papers, Number 69. Salt Lake City: 1964.

The definitive anthropological study of the aboriginal culture of these Indians, with particular reference to the Kaibab band.

MORGAN, DALE L. *Jedediah Smith and the Opening of the West.* New York: Bobbs-Merrill Co., 1953.

This is the best available account of Jed Smith's visit to the Paiute in 1826 and 1827.

STEWARD, JULIAN H. "Notes on Hillers' Photographs of the Paiute and Ute Indians Taken on the Powell Expedition of 1873." *Smithsonian Institution Miscellaneous Collections,* Volume 98, 1939.

While many of the Hillers' historical photographs, such as those reproduced in the present volume, have been reprinted in Euler's *Southern Paiute Ethnohistory,* additional information is presented by Steward.

THE AUTHOR

 ROBERT C. EULER, Professor of Anthropology at Prescott College in Arizona, has carried on extensive archaeological and ethnohistorical research among the Southern Paiute, much of it related to their land claim case. He is a former Chairman of the Department of Anthropology at the University of Utah and has also taught at Northern Arizona University and at Wesleyan University in Connecticut. For several years he was also Curator of Anthropology at the Museum of Northern Arizona in Flagstaff.

Dr. Euler's anthropological research has been done largely among the Indian tribes of the American Southwest and the Great Basin.

He has collaborated with his colleague, Dr. Henry F. Dobyns, in writing two earlier Indian Tribal Series volumes, *The Havasupai People* and *The Hopi People.*

Euler has spent most of his life in the Four Corners country of Utah, Colorado, New Mexico, and Arizona and earned his Ph.D. in anthropology at the University of New Mexico.